This Book Belongs to

www.foxarwen.com

Merch:
www.redbubble.com/people/foxarwen/shop

Collections 2020

Collections 2020

Collections 2020

Collections 2020

Collections 2020

Collections 2020

Collections 2020

Collections 2020

Collections 2020

Collections 2020

Collections 2020

Collections 2020

Holy
Night

Collections 2020

Collections 2020

Collections 2020

Collections 2020

Collections 2020

Collections 2020

Collections 2020

Collections 2020

Collections 2020

Collections 2020

Collections 2020

Collections 2020

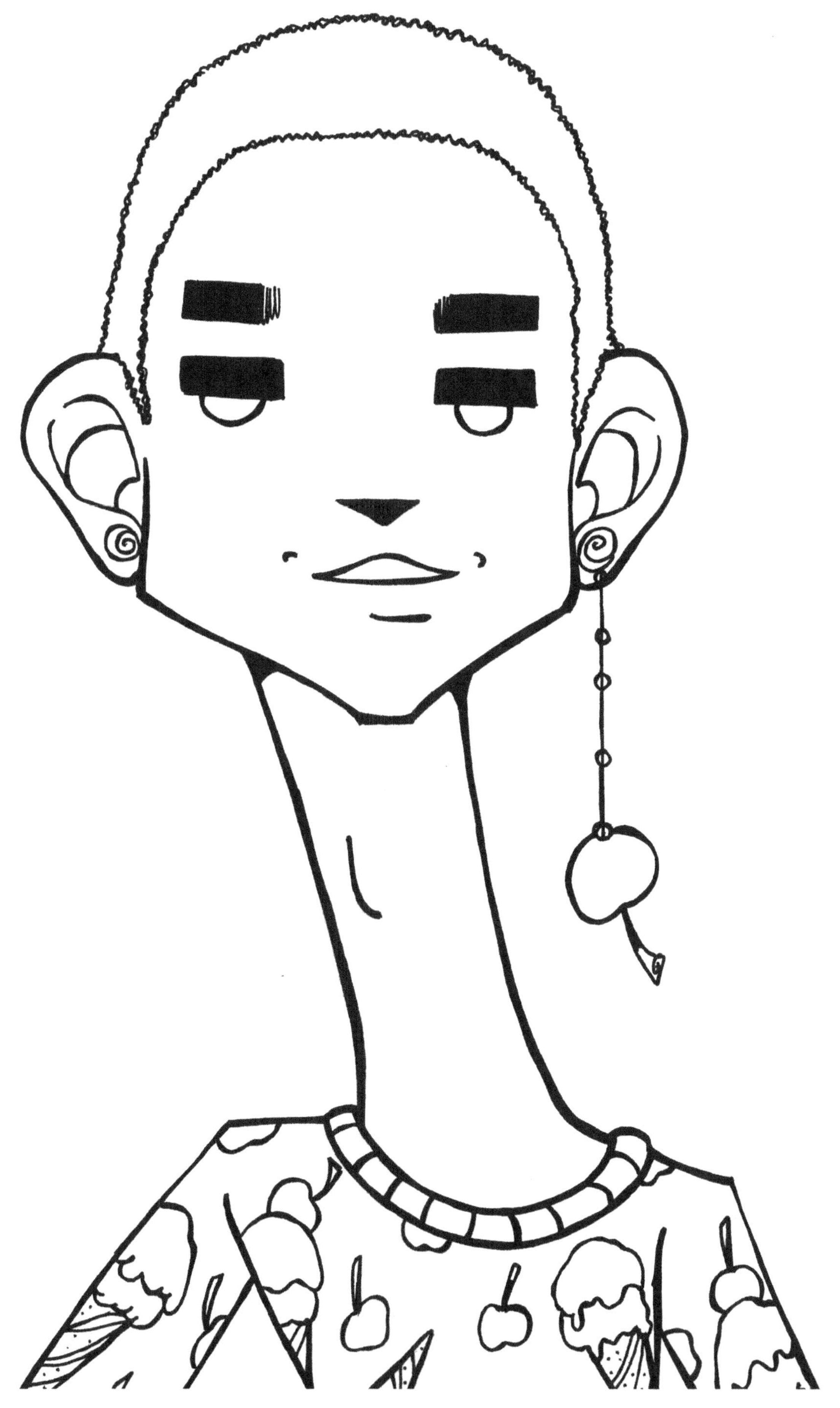

Collections 2020

Collections 2020

Collections 2020

Collections 2020

Collections 2020

Collections 2020

Collections 2020

Collections 2020

Collections 2020

Collections 2020

Collections 2020

Collections 2020

Collections 2020

Collections 2020

Collections 2020

Collections 2020

Colour Swatch Page

Collections 2020